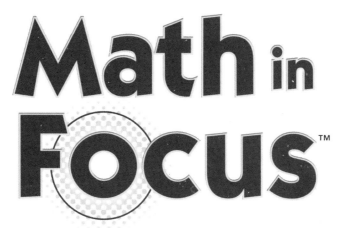

Math in Focus™

The Singapore Approach

Workbook

3A

Consultant and Author
Dr. Fong Ho Kheong

Authors
Chelvi Ramakrishnan and Michelle Choo

U.S. Consultants
Dr. Richard Bisk, Andy Clark,
and Patsy F. Kanter

Marshall Cavendish
Education

GREAT SOURCE®
HOUGHTON MIFFLIN HARCOURT
Supplemental Publishers

© 2009 Marshall Cavendish International (Singapore) Private Limited

Published by Marshall Cavendish Education
An imprint of Marshall Cavendish International (Singapore) Private Limited
A member of Times Publishing Limited

Marshall Cavendish International (Singapore) Private Limited
Times Centre, 1 New Industrial Road
Singapore 536196
Tel: +65 6411 0820
Fax: +65 6266 3677
E-mail: fps@sg.marshallcavendish.com
Website: www.marshallcavendish.com/education

Distributed by
Great Source
A division of Houghton Mifflin Harcourt Publishing Company
181 Ballardvale Street
P.O. Box 7050
Wilmington, MA 01887-7050
Tel: 1-800-289-4490
Website: www.greatsource.com

First published 2009
Reprinted 2010

Math in Focus ™ is a trademark of Times Publishing Limited.

Great Source ® is a registered trademark of Houghton Mifflin Harcourt Publishing Company.

Math in Focus Grade 3 Workbook A
ISBN 978-0-669-01394-8

Printed in Singapore

2 3 4 5 6 7 8   1897   16 15 14 13 12 11 10
4500217576   B C D E

Contents

Addition up to 10,000

Subtraction up to 10,000

5 Using Bar Models: Addition and Subtraction

6 Multiplication Tables of 6, 7, 8, and 9

7 Multiplication

8 Division

Using Bar Models: Multiplication and Division

BLANK

Write each number shown.

— Example —

Thousands	Hundreds	Tens	Ones

$6{,}000 + 600 + 40 + 1 =$ __6,641__

6,000, 600, 40, and 1 make __6,641__.

19.

Thousands	Hundreds	Tens	Ones
	O		

$2{,}000 + 30 + 4 =$ __2,034__

2,000, 30, and 4 make __2,034__.

20.

Thousands	Hundreds	Tens	Ones
	O		0

$3{,}000 + 20 =$ __3,020__

3,000 and 20 make __3,020__.

Complete.

21. $7{,}456 = 7{,}000 + \underline{400} + 50 + 6$

22. $6{,}391 = 6{,}000 + 300 + 90 + \underline{1}$

23. $6{,}193 = 6{,}000 + 100 + \underline{90} + 3$

24. $6{,}107 = 6{,}000 + 100 + \underline{7}$

25. $8{,}904 = \underline{8000} + 900 + 4$

26. $5{,}068 = \underline{5000} + 60 + 8$

27. $9{,}074 = 9{,}000 + \underline{70} + 4$

28. $7{,}005 = 7{,}000 + \underline{5}$

Name: _____ Date: _____

Look for a pattern. Fill in the missing numbers.

25.

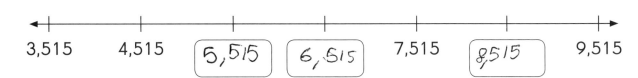

3,515   4,515   [5,515]   [6,515]   7,515   [8,515]   9,515

26.

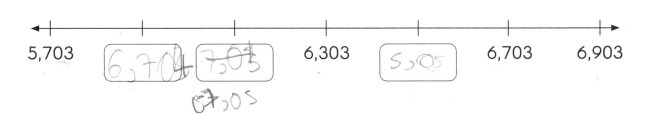

5,703   [6,704 7,503]   6,303   [5,505]   6,703   6,903

07,505

27.

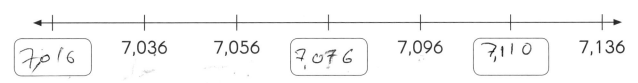

[7,016]   7,036   7,056   [7,076]   7,096   [7,110]   7,136

Complete each number pattern.

28.   _1,755_   _2,755_   _3,755_   5,755   5,765   5,775

29.   8,625   8,725   _9,725_   _10,725_   9,025   9,125

30.   862   962   _1,062_   1,162   1,262   _2,262_

31.   6,315   6,215   6,115   _7,115_   _8,115_   _9,115_

© 2009 Marshall Cavendish International (Singapore) Private Limited

Help Sam follow the correct numbers on the map to get to his mother's office. Write your answers in the boxes.

32. Which is the least: (3,456) 8,265 or 4,456? `3,456`

33. Which is the greatest: 1,978 (1,987) or 1,889? `1,987`

34. Complete the number pattern.

1,980 1,990 __2,000__ 2,010 `2000`

35. Which is less: (8,219) or 8,291?

36. 100 more than 1,912 is __2,012__ .

37. What number is missing?

1,901 1,900 __1,899__ 1,898

Using the numbers in the boxes, color the route that Sam takes to his mother's office.

38. Which office building does he go to?   Office Building Office C Building

Put On Your Thinking Cap!

Challenging Practice

Write the missing number in the pattern.

1.

Thousands	Hundreds	Tens	Ones
5	6	2	3
6	6	2	2
7	6	2	1

Complete each number pattern.

2.   5,621   5,741   5,861   _____

3.   6,871   5,861   _____   3,841

4.   2,828   2,808   2,818   2,798   _____

Fill in the mystery numbers.

5.   I am a 3-digit number. The digit in my tens and ones places is the same. The digit in my hundreds place is 4 more than the digit in my tens and ones places.

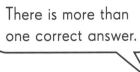

There is more than one correct answer.

I am _____.

Put On Your Thinking Cap!

Problem Solving

I am a 4-digit number.

The digit 8 is in the hundreds place.

The digit in the thousands place is greater than the digit in the hundreds place.

The digit in the ones place is the smallest possible digit.

The digit in the tens place is 3 less than 6.

What number am I?

9830

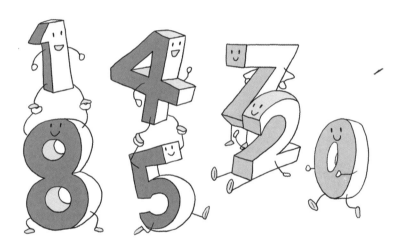

9 8 3 0

Find the sum or difference. Use rounding to check that each answer is reasonable.

┌─── *Example* ───

    $763 + 136 =$ ___899___.

    763 is about ___800___.

    136 is about ___100___.

    ___800___ + ___100___ = ___900___.

    So, $763 + 136$ is about ___900___.

    ___899___ is close to ___900___, so the answer is reasonable.

└───

7. $238 + 598 =$ ___836___.

    238 is about ___300___.

    598 is about ___600___.

    ___300___ + ___600___ = ___900___.

    So, $238 + 598$ is about ___900___.

    ___836___ is close to ___900___, so the answer is reasonable.

8. $846 - 694 =$ ___152___.

    846 is about ___900___.

    694 is about ___600___.

    ___900___ − ___600___ = ___300___.

    So, $846 - 694$ is about ___300___.

    ___152___ is close to ___300___, so the answer is reasonable.

$$\begin{array}{r} {}^1\!8\,{}^1\!4\,6 \\ -\ 6\,9\,4 \\ \hline 1\,5\,2 \end{array}$$

9. 872 − 259 = __113__.

872 is about __800__.

259 is about __300__.

__300__ − __800__ = __500__

So, 872 − 259 is about __500__.

_____ is close to _____, so the answer is reasonable.

$$\begin{array}{r} 8\cancel{7}2 \\ -\ 259 \\ \hline 113 \end{array}$$

10. Mrs. Ramsey wants to buy these four items.

$96 $215 $247 $385

a. Find the total cost of the items.
Then, use rounding to check that the total cost is reasonable.

b. Mrs. Ramsey has $980. Does she have enough money to buy all the items?

10. Find 618 − 372.

618 − 372 = _____

618　　　−　　　372

↓　　　　　　　↓

_____ − _____ = _____

The estimated difference is _____.

The answer _____ is reasonable.

11. Find 936 − 528.

936 − 528 = _____

936　　　−　　　528

↓　　　　　　　↓

_____ − _____ = _____

The estimated difference is _____.

The answer _____ is reasonable.

12. Find 759 − 236.

759 − 236 = _____

759　　　−　　　236

↓　　　　　　　↓

_____ − _____ = _____

The estimated difference is _____.

The answer _____ is reasonable.

Solve.

13. The length of a train engine is 439 centimeters.
The length of the carriage is about 558 centimeters.
Estimate the total length of the train and the carriage.

1,100

439 — 500
558 — 600   +
─────────
1100

14. A wooden pole is 356 centimeters long.
104 centimeters of it is driven into the ground.
About what height of the wooden pole is above the ground? 252

356
− 104
─────
252

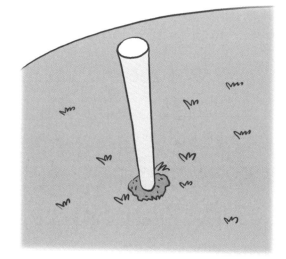

Name: _____   Date: _____

Math Journal

Fill in the blanks that show the steps to add or subtract mentally. You may use the numbers more than once.

1. $35 + 48 = ?$

> **Step 1** Add _____ to _____.
>
> _____ + _____ = _____
>
> **Step 2** Subtract _____ from _____.
>
> _____ − _____ = _____

So, $35 + 48 =$ _____.

subtract
50   83
35
85   2
add

2. $72 - 18 = ?$

> **Step 1** Subtract _____ from _____.
>
> _____ − _____ = _____
>
> **Step 2** Add _____ to _____.
>
> _____ + _____ = _____

So, $72 - 18 =$ _____.

20
add
72   52
subtract
54
2

Complete.

3. Explain how to round 458 to the nearest hundred.
    Include a number line in your explanation.

4. Use front-end estimation to estimate the difference.
    Write the steps to your solution and check that your
    answer is reasonable.

    $905 - 178$

    _____

    _____

    _____

    _____

    _____

5. John used front-end estimation to estimate the sum
    of $317 + 268$.
    Do you agree with his answer? Explain.

    $317 + 268 = 585$

    So, $317 + 268$ is about 600.

    _____

    _____

Put On Your Thinking Cap!

Challenging Practice

1. Two numbers are rounded to the nearest hundred, then added.
    The estimated sum is 500.
    One number is 235. What is the greatest possible value of the other
    number?

2. I am a 3-digit number.
    When you round me to the nearest ten and to the
    nearest hundred, the answer is the same.
    What number can I be?

There are many possible answers.

Put On Your Thinking Cap!

Problem Solving

Mrs. Avilla makes curtains.
She needs 356 centimeters of fabric for the kitchen
and 517 centimeters for the living room.

1.   Estimate the length of the fabric she needs in all by rounding
        to the nearest hundred.

2.   If she buys the length of fabric estimated in Exercise 1, how
        much fabric will be left over?

Put On Your Thinking Cap!

Challenging Practice

Use the digits below. Make as many 4-digit numbers as you can.
Do not begin with '0'.
For each number, use each digit only once.
Then add two 4-digit numbers where you do not need to regroup.

3   5   9   2   0   7

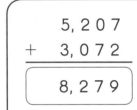

$$5,207$$
$$+\ 3,072$$
$$8,279$$

1.

Now you try it! $3\,2\,5 + 3\,0\,2 = 5$

$3572 + 3025 =$

$$3572$$
$$+3025$$
$$6597$$

Use the digits below. Make as many 4-digit numbers as you can.
Do not begin with '0'.
For each number, use each digit only once.
Then add two 4-digit numbers where you need to regroup.

4   8   1   0   6   9

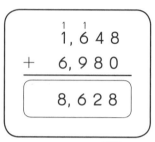

$$\begin{array}{r} \overset{1\ \ 1}{1,648} \\ +\ \ 6,980 \\ \hline 8,628 \end{array}$$

2.

Now you try it!

$$\begin{array}{r} \overset{1}{4}\ 8\ \overset{1}{1}\ 1 \\ 0\ \ 4\ 1\ 1 \\ \hline 5\ 2\ 2\ 2 \end{array}$$

Put On Your Thinking Cap!

Problem Solving

Find the missing numbers.

1.
```
    3, 6  2  5
 +  2, 2 [6] 4
 ─────────────
    5, 8  8  9
```

2.
```
    2, [5] 8  8
 +  3,  6  1  5
 ─────────────
    6,  1  0  3
```

Find the page numbers of the book.

3.

Each of the pages has a 3-digit page number.
The number on Page A is an even number.
The sum of its digits is 7.
The number on Page B is an odd number.
The sum of its digits is 8.
What are the two possible page numbers for
Page A and Page B?

Page 123:
Sum of digits
= 1 + 2 + 3
= 6

Solve.

4. Find two numbers whose sum is 100.

_99_ (+) _1_ = 100

5. Find three numbers whose sum is 150.

_100_ (+) _49_ (+) _1_ = 150

6. A student has four digits.

The digit in (?) is greater than each of the other digits but is less than the sum of these digits.

What is the greatest possible digit? 9

Use the given digits and the answer you found in Exercise 6 to answer Exercises 7 to 9.

7. What is the greatest possible 4-digit number? 1,900

8. What is the least possible 4-digit number? 1,000

9. What is the sum of the 4-digit numbers in Exercises 7 and 8? 4,000

~~1,000~~

Name: _____ Date: _____

Put On Your Thinking Cap!

Problem Solving

Solve. Show your work.

1. The difference between two numbers is 100.
One number is more than 90 but less than 100.
The other number is between 190 and 200.
What are the two possible numbers?

_____ and _____

2. Lilian went shopping with $1,000.
She saw five items on display in a shop window.
After buying two items, she had $732 left.
Which two items did she buy?

_____ and _____

Solve.

3. Nick and Isaac are at a school fair.
They want to collect points to exchange for these prizes.

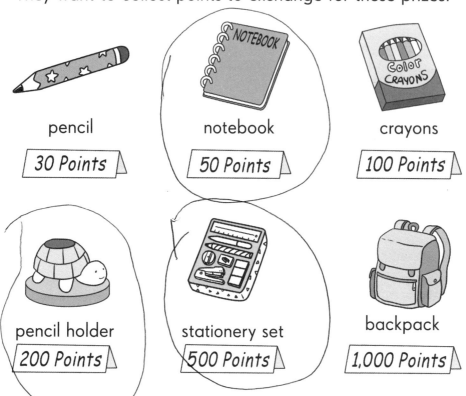

pencil
30 Points

notebook
50 Points

crayons
100 Points

pencil holder
200 Points

stationery set
500 Points

backpack
1,000 Points

At the fair games, Nick has 215 points and Isaac has 78 points.
They combine their points to exchange for three prizes.
What are the two sets of three prizes they can get?

a. _____

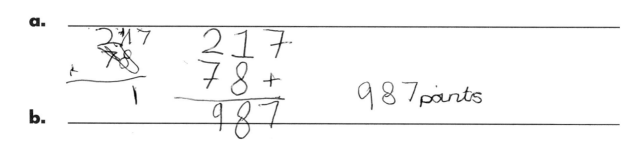

$$\begin{array}{r} 2\;1\;7 \\ 7\;8\;+ \\ \hline 9\;8\;7 \end{array}$$

987 points

b. _____

Practice 2   Real-World Problems:
Addition and Subtraction

Solve. Draw bar models to help you.

Example

Janice has 1,458 stamps.
She has 396 fewer stamps than Ben.

a.   How many stamps does Ben have?

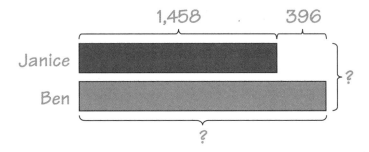

$\underline{\quad 1,458 \quad}$ ⊕ $\underline{\quad 396 \quad}$ = $\underline{\quad 1,854 \quad}$

Ben has $\underline{\quad 1,854 \quad}$ stamps.

b.   How many stamps do they have in all?

$\underline{\quad 1,458 \quad}$ ⊕ $\underline{\quad 1,854 \quad}$ = $\underline{\quad 3,312 \quad}$

They have $\underline{\quad 3,312 \quad}$ stamps in all.

Solve. Draw bar models to help you.

1. There are 1,287 men at a baseball game.
There are 879 fewer women than men at the game.

   a. How many women are at the game?

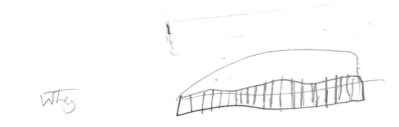

_____ ◯ _____ = _____

_____ women are at the game.

   b. How many adult spectators are at the game?

_____ ◯ _____ = _____

_____ adult spectators are at the game.

Solve. Draw bar models to help you.

4.   Mr. Tuzamoto's factory makes 1,793 toys each day.
It makes 157 more toys than Ms. Jefferson's factory.

    a.   How many toys does Ms. Jefferson's factory make each day?

    Ms. Jefferson's factory makes _____ toys each day.

    b.   If Ms. Jefferson's factory sells 698 toys, how many toys does her factory have left?

    Ms. Jefferson's factory has _____ toys left.

Solve. Draw bar models to help you.

5. A middle school has 3,756 students.
It has 455 fewer students than an elementary school.

  a. How many students does the elementary school have?

  b. How many students do both schools have in all?

Name: _kyla_ **Date:** _____

Practice 3 Real-World Problems: Addition and Subtraction

Solve. Draw bar models to help you.

─ *Example* ─

Jake mixes 620 liters of water and
180 liters of syrup to make lemonade.
He adds another 145 liters of water to the mixture.
How much more water than syrup does he use
for the lemonade?

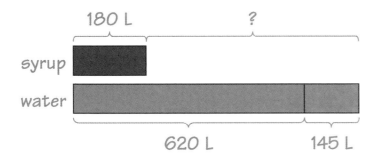

620 + 145 = 765

He uses 765 liters of water.

765 – 180 = 585

He uses 585 liters more water than syrup.

Solve. Draw bar models to help you.

1. A pet store donates 3,500 pounds of dog food to an animal shelter.
    A farm donates 2,500 pounds of dog food at first.
    Later it donates another 2,000 pounds of dog food to the animal shelter.
    How many more pounds of dog food does the farm donate than the pet store? $\subseteq$ 5000

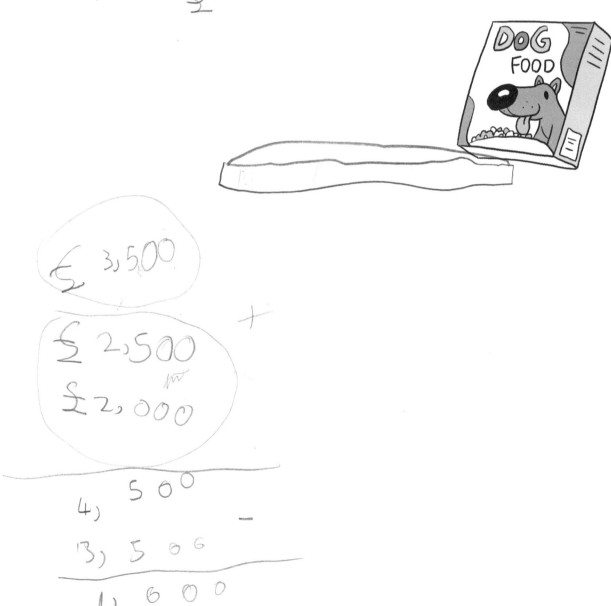

$\subseteq$ 3,500

$\subseteq$ 2,500
$\subseteq$ 2,000 +

$$4,500$$
$$-3,500$$
$$1,600$$

Math Journal

Write your own real-world problem.
Solve. Draw bar models to help you.

> The Park Fund
> raises $2,960.
> The Playground
> Fund raises $2,662.

> The Park Fund raises $298 more
> than the Playground Fund.
> The Playground Fund raises $298
> less than the Park Fund.
> The Park Fund and the Playground
> Fund raise $5,622 in all.

Example

Word problem

The Park Fund raises $2,960.
The Playground Fund raises $298 less than the Park Fund.
How much does the Playground Fund raise?

Model

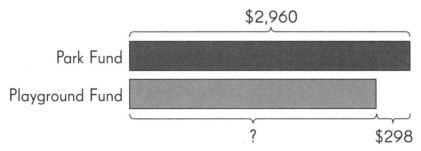

Solution

$2,960 − $298 = $2,662

The Playground Fund raises $2,662.

Now you try it!

Word problem

Model

Solution

 Put On Your Thinking Cap!

 Challenging Practice

Look at the cards.

318	456	195
A	B	C

Think of three ways to choose two cards.
Find the sum of the two cards.

> *Example*
>
> A and B; ____318____ + ____456____ = ____774____

1. _____ and _____ ; _____ + _____ = _____

2. _____ and _____ ; _____ + _____ = _____

Fill in the missing letters.

3. Which two cards give the greatest sum? _____ and _____

4. Which two cards give the least sum? _____ and _____

5. Which two cards give the greatest difference? _____ and _____

6. Which two cards give the least difference? _____ and _____

Put On Your Thinking Cap!

Problem Solving

1. Carlos has been collecting cards since he was 5 years old.
    He has not thrown away any of his cards.
    He is now 7 years old.
    He collected 201 cards last year.
    He collects 125 cards this year.
    He has a total of 589 cards now.

    a. How many cards did he have in total at the end of last year?
    b. How many cards did he collect when he was 5 years old?

2. Jason, Peter, and Ken hold a garage sale for charity.
    Jason raises $350.
    Peter raises $20 more than Jason.
    Ken raises the same amount as the total amount raised by Jason and Peter.

    How much money do the three boys raise in all?

Cumulative Review

for Chapters 3 to 5

Concepts and Skills

Add. *(Lessons 3.1, 3.2, and 3.3)*

1.
$$\begin{array}{r} 6,305 \\ +\ 2,512 \\ \hline \boxed{4,913} \end{array}$$

2.
$$\begin{array}{r} 3,100 \\ +\ 2,800 \\ \hline \boxed{1,700} \end{array}$$

Subtract. *(Lessons 4.1, 4.2 and 4.3)*

3.
$$\begin{array}{r} 8,754 \\ -\ \ \ 531 \\ \hline \boxed{8,223} \end{array}$$

4.
$$\begin{array}{r} 78,615 \\ -\ 2,704 \\ \hline \boxed{5,911} \end{array}$$

Fill in the missing numbers.

5.
$$\begin{array}{r} \boxed{4},265 \\ +\ 2,058 \\ \hline 6,323 \end{array}$$

6.
$$\begin{array}{r} 4,672 \\ +\ 3,\boxed{5}79 \\ \hline 8,251 \end{array}$$

7.
$$\begin{array}{r} 2,\boxed{5}61 \\ -\ \ \ 684 \\ \hline 1,877 \end{array}$$

8.
$$\begin{array}{r} 5,010 \\ -\ \boxed{1}685 \\ \hline 1,325 \end{array}$$

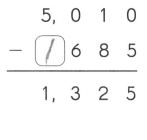

Complete. *(Lesson 4.4)*

9.   Gabriel and Sue are at an amusement park.

    a.   Gabriel throws two darts at a target board.
        The difference between the two numbers is 75.
        Circle the two numbers.

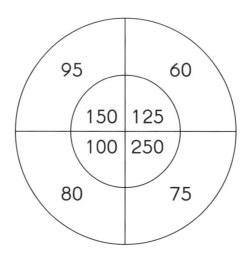

    b.   Sue throws two darts at another target board.
        The difference between the two numbers is 2,700.
        Circle the two numbers.

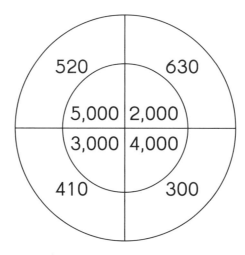

Problem Solving

Solve. Draw bar models to help you. *(Lesson 5.1)*

10. 5,476 people ride Bus D in March.
1,496 fewer people ride Bus E in the same month.
  a. How many people ride Bus E in March?
  b. How many people ride both buses in March?

11. A supermarket has 1,213 apples.
368 are green apples.
  a. How many of the apples are red?
  b. How many more red apples than green apples does the
supermarket have?

12. 2,500 people visit the Children's Museum on Monday.
On Tuesday, there were 532 more people at the museum than on Monday.
What is the total number of visitors for both days?

13. Michael has 754 songs in his audio device.
He has 98 more songs than Peter.
How many songs do they have in all?

Practice 3   Multiply by 7

Look at each area model. Write the multiplication fact.

Example

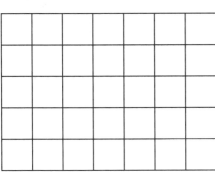

_____5_____ × _____7_____ = _____35_____

1.

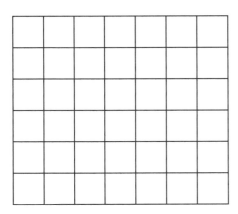

_____ × _____ = _____

2.

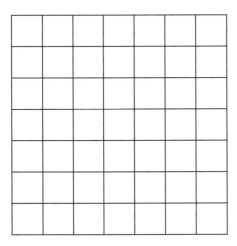

_____ × _____ = _____

Fill in the missing numbers.

3.   6 sevens $= 6 \times$ ___7___ ✓

4. $9 \times 7 =$ ___63___ sevens

5. $5 + 5 + 5 + 5 + 5 + 5 + 5 = 7 \times$ ___~~28~~___ 35

6. $7 + 7 + 7 + 7 + 7 = 5 \times$ ___~~35~~ 7___ ✓

7. $10 \times 7 = 7 \times$ ___10___ ✓

8.   4 sevens $= 7 + 7 + 7 +$ ___~~28~~ 7___ ✓

Multiply. Use multiplication facts you know to find other multiplication facts.

9. $7 \times 4 = 5$ groups of $4 +$ _____ groups of 4

           $=$ _____ $+$ _____

           $=$ _____

10. $5 \times 7 =$ _____

        $7 \times 7 = 5$ groups of $7 +$ _____ groups of 7

           $=$ _____ $+$ _____

           $=$ _____

11. $10 \times 7 =$ _____

        $9 \times 7 = 10$ groups of $7 -$ _____ group of 7

           $=$ _____ $-$ _____

           $=$ _____

Multiply and match.

12.

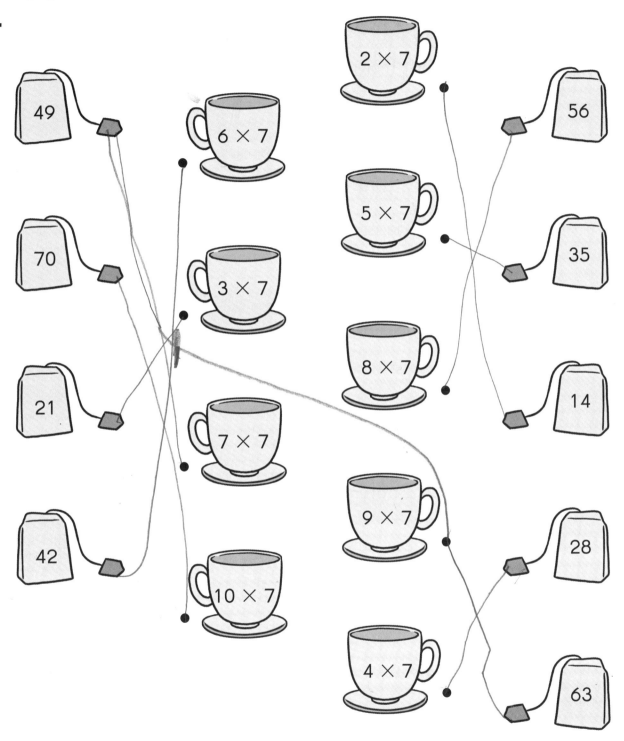

It is a......

Solve.

13.   Mrs. Thompson buys 2 books.
Each book costs $7.
How much does Mrs. Thompson pay in all?

$2 \times \$7 = \$$_____

Mrs. Thompson pays $\$$_____ in all.

14.   A box contains 7 crayons.
Alex packs 10 such boxes into his bag.
How many crayons does Alex have in all?

$10 \times 7 =$ _____

Alex has _____ crayons in all.

15.   Mr. Dean gives each student 7 okras in art class.
How many okras does he give 4 students?

$4 \times 7 =$ _____

He gives 4 students _____ okras.

Practice 5   Multiply by 9

Complete the multiplication fact. Then show on the number line.

1. $2 \times 9 =$ _____

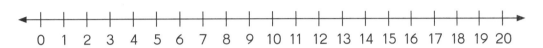

Complete the multiplication fact. Then show on the area model.

2. $7 \times 9 =$ _____

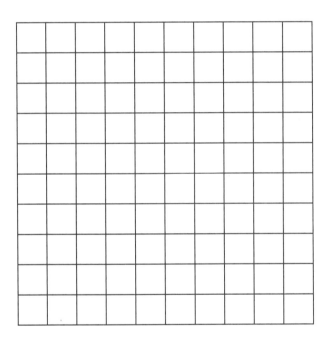

Fill in the missing numbers.

3.   3 nines $= 3 \times$ _____

4.   4 nines $=$ _____ $\times 9$

Fill in the missing numbers.

5. $9 + 9 + 9 + 9 + 9 + 9 = 6 \times$ _____

6. $6 + 6 + 6 + 6 + 6 + 6 + 6 + 6 + 6 = 9 \times$ _____

7. $9 \times 8 = 8 \times$ _____

8. 8 nines $= 9 + 9 + 9 + 9 + 9 + 9 +$ _____ $+$ _____

Use multiplication facts to help you.

9. $10 \times 4 =$ _____

$9 \times 4 = 10$ groups of $4 -$ _____ group of 4

$=$ _____ $-$ _____

$=$ _____

10. $10 \times 9 =$ _____

$9 \times 9 = 10$ groups of $9 -$ _____ group of 9

$=$ _____ $-$ _____

$=$ _____

11. $5 \times 9 =$ _____

$6 \times 9 = 5$ groups of $9 +$ _____ group of 9

$=$ _____ $+$ _____

$=$ _____

Name: _____ Date: _____

Match each ball to the correct basket.

12.

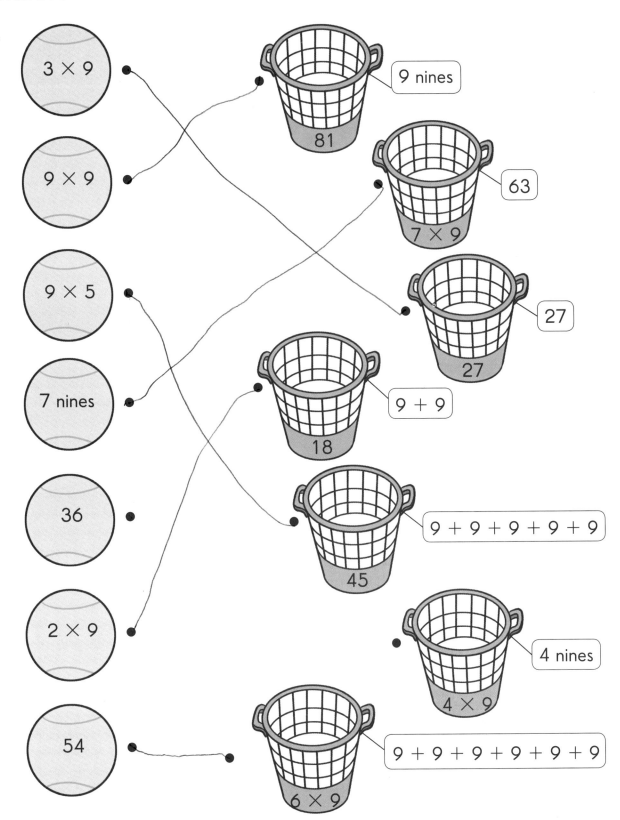

Solve.

13. Pamela pastes stickers on 4 cards.
She pastes 9 stickers on each card.
How many stickers does she paste in all?

_____ × 9 = _____

She pastes _____ stickers in all.

Use the pictures to write a multiplication story.

14.

scissors
$6

marker
$4

pencil
$2

_____

_____

_____

_____

Practice 6   Division: Finding the Number of Items in Each Group

Write two related division sentences.

> *Example*
>
> $6 \times 7 = 42$
>
> $42 \div \underline{\quad 6 \quad} = \underline{\quad 7 \quad}$
>
> $42 \div \underline{\quad 7 \quad} = \underline{\quad 6 \quad}$

1. $9 \times 5 = 45$

$45 \div \underline{\qquad\quad} = \underline{\qquad\quad}$

$45 \div \underline{\qquad\quad} = \underline{\qquad\quad}$

2. $7 \times 9 = 63$

$63 \div \underline{\qquad\quad} = \underline{\qquad\quad}$

$63 \div \underline{\qquad\quad} = \underline{\qquad\quad}$

3. $8 \times 6 = 48$

$48 \div \underline{\qquad\quad} = \underline{\qquad\quad}$

$48 \div \underline{\qquad\quad} = \underline{\qquad\quad}$

Fill in the missing numbers.

> *Example*
>
> $6 \times$ _____7_____ $= 42$ So, $42 \div 6 =$ _____7_____.

4. $7 \times$ _____ $= 49$ So, $49 \div 7 =$ _____.

5. $8 \times$ _____ $= 48$ So, $48 \div 8 =$ _____.

6. $9 \times$ _____ $= 45$ So, $45 \div 9 =$ _____.

Solve.

7.   Mrs. Brown has 9 purses with 54 coins.
Each purse has the same number of coins.
How many coins does each purse have?

_____ $\div$ _____ $=$ _____

Each purse has _____ coins.

8.   Austin collects 63 seashells.
He puts them equally into 7 boxes.
How many seashells does each box contain?

_____ $\div$ _____ $=$ _____

Each box contains _____ seashells.

Practice 7   Division: Making Equal Groups

Fill in the missing numbers.

1. _____ × 6 = 54   **2.** _____ × 8 = 56

54 ÷ 6 = _____   56 ÷ 8 = _____

Divide.

3. 21 ÷ 7 = _____   **4.** 72 ÷ 8 = _____

5. 63 ÷ 9 = _____   **6.** 48 ÷ 6 = _____

Solve.

7. One tank holds 8 gallons of water.
How many tanks are needed to hold 64 gallons of water?

_____ ÷ _____ = _____

_____ tanks are needed to hold 64 gallons of water.

8. Donald packs 36 apples into some bags.
Each bag contains 9 apples.
How many bags does Donald use?

_____ ÷ _____ = _____

Donald uses _____ bags.

 Math Journal

1. Show 3 × 6 on the number line.

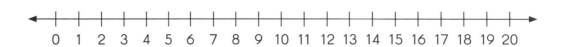

0 1 2 3 4 5 6 7 8 9 10 11 12 13 14 15 16 17 18 19 20

2. Draw an array model to show 5 × 7.

3. Show 8 × 9 with the area model.

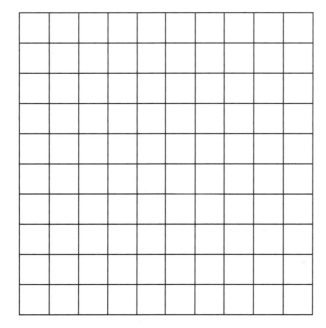

Put On Your Thinking Cap!

 Challenging Practice

Complete each skip-counting pattern.

1. 70 63 56 _____ _____ 35

_____ _____ 14 7

2. 80 72 64 _____ _____ _____

_____ _____ 16 8

Identify a number that does not belong in the group.
Then write the reason.
Use the number patterns to help you.

3.

Number: _____

Reason: _____

_____

_____

4.

Number: _____

Reason: _____

_____

_____

 Put On Your Thinking Cap!

Problem Solving

1. I am a two-digit number.
I am less than 50.
Count in sixes and you will find me!
Divide my tens digit by 2 and you will find my ones digit.
What am I?

Make a systematic list as shown below to help you.

Number	Tens Digit	Ones Digit	Check
12	1	2	✗
12 + 6 =			

I am _____.

Chapter 7 Multiplication

Practice 1 Mental Multiplication

Multiply mentally. Fill in the missing numbers.

Example

Find 4×7.

4×7 is the same as 7×4.

So, $4 \times 7 = \underline{\quad 28 \quad}$.

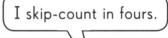

I skip-count in fours.

1. Find 3×9.

  3×9 is the same as 9×3.

  So, $3 \times 9 = \underline{\qquad\qquad}$.

2. Find 5×7.

  5×7 is the same as 7×5.

  So, $5 \times 7 = \underline{\qquad\qquad}$.

3. Find 9×8.

  9×8 is the same as 8×9.

  So, $9 \times 8 = \underline{\qquad\qquad}$.

Multiply mentally. Fill in the missing numbers.

Example

$$3 \times 50 = 3 \times 5 \text{ tens}$$
$$= \underline{\quad 15 \quad} \text{ tens}$$
$$= \underline{\quad 150 \quad}$$

4. $3 \times 500 = 3 \times 5 \text{ hundreds}$

$= \underline{\hspace{2cm}} \text{ hundreds}$

$= \underline{\hspace{2cm}}$

5. $7 \times 40 = 7 \times 4 \text{ tens}$

$= \underline{\hspace{2cm}} \text{ tens}$

$= \underline{\hspace{2cm}}$

6. $7 \times 400 = 7 \times 4 \text{ hundreds}$

$= \underline{\hspace{2cm}} \text{ hundreds}$

$= \underline{\hspace{2cm}}$

7. $8 \times 60 = 8 \times 6 \text{ tens}$

$= \underline{\hspace{2cm}} \text{ tens}$

$= \underline{\hspace{2cm}}$

8. $8 \times 600 = 8 \times 6 \text{ hundreds}$

$= \underline{\hspace{2cm}} \text{ hundreds}$

$= \underline{\hspace{2cm}}$

Multiply mentally.

9. $9 \times 20 = \underline{\hspace{2cm}}$

10. $9 \times 200 = \underline{\hspace{2cm}}$

11. $2 \times 70 = \underline{\hspace{2cm}}$

12. $2 \times 700 = \underline{\hspace{2cm}}$

13. $8 \times 30 = \underline{\hspace{2cm}}$

14. $8 \times 300 = \underline{\hspace{2cm}}$

Multiply.

Example

$$
\begin{array}{r}
4\ 1\ 4 \\
\times\quad 2 \\
\hline
\boxed{8\ 2\ 8}
\end{array}
$$

4.
$$
\begin{array}{r}
3\ 2\ 1 \\
\times\quad 3 \\
\hline
\end{array}
$$

5.
$$
\begin{array}{r}
1\ 0\ 2 \\
\times\quad 4 \\
\hline
\end{array}
$$

6.
$$
\begin{array}{r}
1\ 0\ 1 \\
\times\quad 5 \\
\hline
\end{array}
$$

Match each caterpillar to its leaf.

7.

646

408

603

888

201×3

323×2

222×4

102×4

Multiply and complete.

8. Frederick Frog is hungry.
He is out hunting for his lunch.
Clever Frederick Frog eats only non-poisonous flies.
Flies carrying a product greater than 400 are non-poisonous.
Which flies should Frederick Frog eat?

Frederick Frog should eat flies _____.

Solve.

┌─ *Example* ───┐

Curtis scores 22 points in a game.
He wants to score the same number of points for every game.
How many points does he hope to score in 4 games?

$22 \times 4 = 88$

$$\begin{array}{r} 2\ 2 \\ \times\ \ \ \ 4 \\ \hline 8\ 8 \end{array}$$

He hopes to score 88 points in 4 games.

└───┘

9. 143 people ride the train every hour.
How many people ride the train in 2 hours?

10. A bakery sells 213 muffins a day.
How many muffins does it sell in 3 days?

11. A website has 232 hits in the first week.
In the second week, the website has the same number of hits.
How many hits does the website have in both weeks?

12. A grocery store sells 202 cartons of milk a week.
How many cartons of milk does it sell in 4 weeks?

Fill in the missing numbers.

6. $5 \times 145 = ?$

$$\begin{array}{r} \boxed{}\boxed{} \\ 1 \quad 4 \quad 5 \\ \times \qquad 5 \\ \hline \boxed{} \end{array}$$

Step 1   Multiply the ones by 5.

$5 \times$ _____ ones = _____ ones

Regroup the ones.

_____ ones = _____ tens _____ ones

Step 2   Multiply the tens by 5.

$5 \times$ _____ tens = _____ tens

Add the tens.

_____ tens + _____ tens = _____ tens

Regroup the tens.

_____ tens = _____ hundreds _____ tens

Step 3   Multiply the hundreds by 5.

$5 \times$ _____ hundred = _____ hundreds

Add the hundreds.

_____ hundreds + _____ hundreds

= _____ hundreds

So, $5 \times 145 =$ _____.

Fill in the missing numbers.

7.   5 × 159 = ?

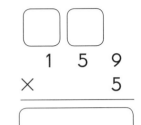

	1	5	9
×			5

Step 1   Multiply the ones by 5.

5 × _____ ones = _____ ones

Regroup the ones.

_____ ones = _____ tens _____ ones

Step 2   Multiply the tens by 5.

5 × _____ tens = _____ tens

Add the tens.

_____ tens + _____ tens = _____ tens

Regroup the tens.

_____ tens = _____ hundreds _____ tens

Step 3   Multiply the hundreds by 5.

5 × _____ hundred = _____ hundreds

Add the hundreds.

_____ hundreds + _____ hundreds

= _____ hundreds

So, 5 × 159 = _____.

Practice 4   Multiplying Ones, Tens, and Hundreds with Regrouping

Multiply and complete.

1.

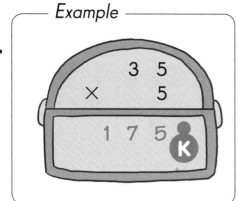

Example

$$
\begin{array}{r}
3\ 5 \\
\times\quad 5 \\
\hline
1\ 7\ 5 \\
\end{array}
$$
K

$$
\begin{array}{r}
4\ 8\ 6 \\
\times\quad 2 \\
\hline
9\ 7\ 2 \\
\end{array}
$$
D

$$
\begin{array}{r}
2\ 7\ 9 \\
\times\quad 3 \\
\hline
8\ 3\ 7 \\
\end{array}
$$
Y

$$
\begin{array}{r}
2\ 9\ 7 \\
\times\quad 3 \\
\hline
6\ 9\ 1 \\
\end{array}
$$
A

$$
\begin{array}{r}
3\ 0\ 4 \\
\times\quad 3 \\
\hline
9\ 3\ 2 \\
\end{array}
$$
L

$$
\begin{array}{r}
1\ 5\ 6 \\
\times\quad 4 \\
\hline
6\ 2\ 4 \\
\end{array}
$$
O

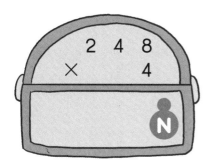

$$
\begin{array}{r}
2\ 4\ 8 \\
\times\quad 4 \\
\hline
\end{array}
$$
N

$$
\begin{array}{r}
1\ 5\ 5 \\
\times\quad 5 \\
\hline
\end{array}
$$
Z

$$
\begin{array}{r}
1\ 9\ 9 \\
\times\quad 5 \\
\hline
\end{array}
$$
E

What key cannot unlock treasure chests?

Write the letters which match the answers to find out.

D	O	N	K	E	Y
972	624	992	175	995	837

Solve.

> *Example*
>
> Gina reads 84 pages of her book in a day.
> How many pages does Gina read in 5 days?
>
> $84 \times 5 = 420$
>
> Gina reads 420 pages in 5 days.

2. 187 cars are in a parking lot.
Each car has 4 wheels.
How many wheels do the cars have in all?

3. 198 students attend a school.
Each student carries 3 books.
How many books do they carry in all?

4. Jill feeds her pet hamster 5 food pellets each day.
How many food pellets does she feed her hamster in 165 days?

Multiply.

5.   450 × 2 = _____   **6.**   232 × 4 = _____

7.   259 × 3 = _____   **8.**   196 × 5 = _____

Complete.

9.   Circle the chest with the greatest product.

10.   Underline the chest with the least product.

Solve.
Then circle the chest with the correct answer.

11.   Keith runs from Tree A to B to C, to D to E, then to F.
           The trees are planted 134 meters apart from each other.
           How far does Keith run in all?

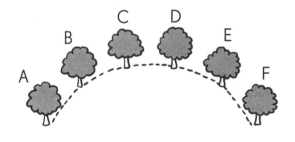

Keith runs _____ meters in all.

Math Journal

Write the steps to your answer.

Multiply 243 by 2.

Example

Step 1	Multiply 3 ones by 2.	2 4 3
	2×3 ones = 6 ones	$\times$ 2
		6

Step 2	Multiply 4 tens by 2.	2 4 3
	2×4 tens = 8 tens	$\times$ 2
		8 6

Step 3	Multiply 2 hundreds by 2.	2 4 3
	2×2 hundreds = 4 hundreds	$\times$ 2

So, $2 \times 243 = 486$.

4 8 6

Multiply 323 by 3.

$$\begin{array}{r} 3\ 2\ 3 \\ \times \quad\ 3 \\ \hline \end{array}$$

Step 1 _____

_____

Step 2 _____

_____

Step 3 _____

_____

Name: _____ Date: _____

 Put On Your Thinking Cap!

 Challenging Practice

Fill in the missing numbers.

1.

```
  2 [4]
×   2
─────
  4 8
```

   24
2√48

2.

```
  1 7
×  [ ]
─────
  6 8
```

3.

```
 [2] 3 1
×     3
───────
  6 9 3
```

   231
3√693

4.

```
  1 2 1
×    [ ]
───────
  6 0 5
```

5.

```
  3 0 8
×   [2]
───────
  6 1 6
```

   300
   300
   6√6
  ─────
  × 6

   616

300√616

6.

```
  1 [ ] 5
×      4
───────
  5 4 0
```

7.

```
 [ ] 5 2
×     3
───────
  7 5 6
```

8.

```
  1 [ ] 8
×      4
───────
  5 9 2
```

   758
   52+
  ─────
   868

   122
3√756

Put On Your Thinking Cap!

Problem Solving

Solve.

Frank has 100 geese and cows on his farm.
The animals have a total of 340 legs.
How many geese and cows does Frank have?

Guess and check
your answer.

Geese (2 legs)	Cows (4 legs)	Total number of legs	Correct (✓) / Wrong (✗)
50 × 2 = 100	50 × 4 = 200	100 + 200 = 300	✗
60 × 2 = 120	40 × 4 = 160	120 + 160 = 280	✗

Frank has _____ geese and _____ cows.

Cumulative Review

for Chapters 6 and 7

Concepts and Skills

Fill in the blanks. *(Lessons 6.1 to 6.5)*

1. _____ $\times 8 = 0$

2. _____ $\times 1 = 7$

3. $9 \text{ sixes} = 9 \times$ _____

4. $4 \times 7 =$ _____ sevens

5. $3 \times 6 = 6 + 6 +$ _____

6. $7 \times 6 = 6 \times$ _____

7. $9 \times$ _____ $= 0$

8. $8 + 8 + 8 + 8 + 8 = 5 \times$ _____

9. $5 \text{ nines} + 3 \text{ nines} =$ _____ $\times 9$

10. $9 + 9 + 9 + 9 =$ _____ nines

Complete each multiplication fact.
Then show on the number line. *(Lessons 6.1 and 6.4)*

11. $2 \times 4 \times 3 = ?$

Step 1   _____ $\times\ 4 =$ _____

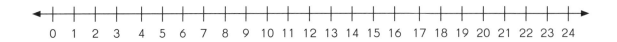

Step 2   _____ $\times\ 3 =$ _____

So, $2 \times 4 \times 3 =$ _____ $\times$ _____

= _____ .

12. $2 \times 4 \times 3 = ?$

Step 1   _____ $\times\ 3 =$ _____

Step 2 $2 \times$ _____ = _____

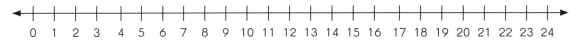

So, $2 \times 4 \times 3 =$ _____ $\times$ _____

= _____ .

Multiply. Use multiplication facts you know to find other multiplication facts. *(Lessons 6.3 and 6.5)*

13. $5 \times 7 =$ _____

So, $6 \times 7 =$ _____ groups of 7 + _____ group of 7

$=$ _____ + _____

$=$ _____

14. $10 \times 9 =$ _____

So, $8 \times 9 =$ _____ groups of 9 − _____ groups of 9

$=$ _____ − _____

$=$ _____

Write two related division sentences. *(Lessons 6.3, 6.4, 6.5 and 6.6)*

15. $8 \times 4 =$ _____

_____ ÷ _____ = _____

_____ ÷ _____ = _____

16. _____ × _____ = _____

$54 ÷$ _____ $= 9$

_____ ÷ _____ = _____

Multiply. Fill in the missing numbers. *(Lesson 7.1)*

17. $4 \times 9 = $ _____

$4 \times 90 = 4 \times$ _____ tens

$=$ _____ tens

$=$ _____

18. $10 \times 7 = $ _____

$10 \times 700 = 10 \times$ _____ hundreds

$=$ _____ hundreds

$=$ _____

Multiply. Use mental math. *(Lesson 7.1)*

19. $10 \times 3 = $ _____

20. $5 \times 10 = $ _____

21. $20 \times 4 = $ _____

22. $3 \times 40 = $ _____

23. $500 \times 2 = $ _____

24. $4 \times 200 = $ _____

Multiply. Show your work. *(Lessons 7.2 and 7.3)*

25. $212 \times 4 = $ _____

26. $148 \times 5 = $ _____

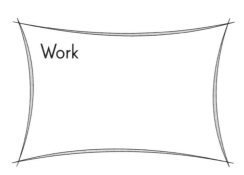

Work

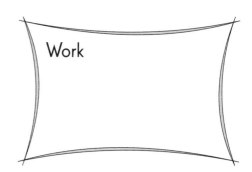

Work

27.

$$\begin{array}{r} 4\ 3\ 2 \\ \times \quad\quad 2 \\ \hline \end{array}$$

28.

$$\begin{array}{r} 2\ 5\ 1 \\ \times \quad\quad 3 \\ \hline \end{array}$$

Problem Solving

Solve. Show your work.

29. Cheryl completes 42 pages of math exercises.
There are 4 exercises on each page.
How many exercises does she complete?

30. Damien has 48 marbles.
He packs all the marbles equally into 8 bags.
How many marbles are there in each bag?

31. Mr. Roberts has 63 daisies and some pots.
He plants 9 daisies in each pot.
How many pots does he use?

32. A farmer packs 49 pounds of grain into 7-pound bags.
How many bags does the farmer need?

33. A grocer sells 153 bags of carrots.
Each bag has 5 carrots.
How many carrots does the grocer sell?

34. Jessie buys 4 cartons of markers.
Each carton contains 125 markers.
How many markers does she buy?

Division

Practice 1   Mental Division

Think of the multiplication facts for 6, 7, 8, and 9.
Then fill in the blanks.

> *Example*
>
> _____*6*_____ × 6 = 36   36 ÷ 6 = _____*6*_____

1. _____ × 7 = 35   35 ÷ 7 = _____

2. _____ × 8 = 72   72 ÷ 8 = _____

3. _____ × 9 = 63   63 ÷ 9 = _____

4. _____ × 9 = 81   81 ÷ 9 = _____

Fill in the blanks.

5. $56 \div 7 =$ ___56___ ones $\div 7$

   $=$ ___8___ ones

   $=$ ___8___

6. $360 \div 9 =$ ___036___ tens $\div 9$

   $=$ ___4___ tens

   $=$ ___40___

7. $600 \div 3 =$ ___6___ hundreds $\div 3$

   $=$ ___2.00___ hundreds

   $=$ ___200___

8. $4,500 \div 5 =$ ___45___ hundreds $\div 5$

   $=$ ___900___ hundreds

   $=$ ___900___

Divide. Use related multiplication facts and patterns to help you.

9. $240 \div 4 =$ ___60___   10. $250 \div 5 =$ ___50___

11. $180 \div 9 =$ ___20___   12. $180 \div 6 =$ ___30___

13. $320 \div 8 =$ ___40___   14. $490 \div 7 =$ ___70___

Name: Kyla 1234 6 2 8 10 11   **Date:** _____

Practice 3   Odd and Even Numbers

Look at the picture. Then answer the question.
Explain your answer.

1.   Is 21 an even number? ___no___

Explain your answer.

___because 1 3 5 7 9 is odd.___

2.   Is 32 an odd number? ___no___

Explain your answer.

___because 2 4 6 8 10 is even___

Divide.

3. $14 \div 2 =$ [7] R [0]

4. $23 \div 2 =$ [▨] R [0]

5. $29 \div 2 =$ [   ] R [   ]

Use your answers in Questions 3, 4, and 5 to answer
Questions 6 and 7.

6.   _____ is an even number.

It does not have a _____ when divided by 2.

7.   _____ and _____ are odd numbers.

They have a _____ of _____ when divided by 2.

Look at the numbers in the box. Then answer the questions.

11	30	68	76	59	95
84	92	123	477	980	

8.   Circle the **even numbers** and write them on the line below.

_____

9.   Write the **odd numbers**. _____

10.   Write the ones digit in the even numbers in Question 8. _____

11.   Write the ones digit in the odd numbers in Question 9. _____

Fill in the blanks.

12.   Use the digits to make the
greatest 4-digit **odd number**.   4   5   2   9   _____

13.   Use the digits to make the
least 4-digit **even number**.   0   1   6   9   _____
(Do not begin with zero.)

Practice 4 Division Without Remainder and Regrouping

Divide. Then match the answers to the correct pictures.

Tens	Ones

1. 44 ones ÷ 4 = _____ ten _____ one •   •

2. 69 ones ÷ 3 = _____ tens _____ ones •   •

Tens	Ones

Divide.

3.

$3 \overline{)36}$

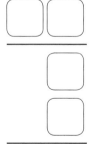

4.

$4 \overline{)84}$

5.

$5 \overline{)55}$

Divide.
Then draw a line from each tree to the bird with the matching quotient.

6.

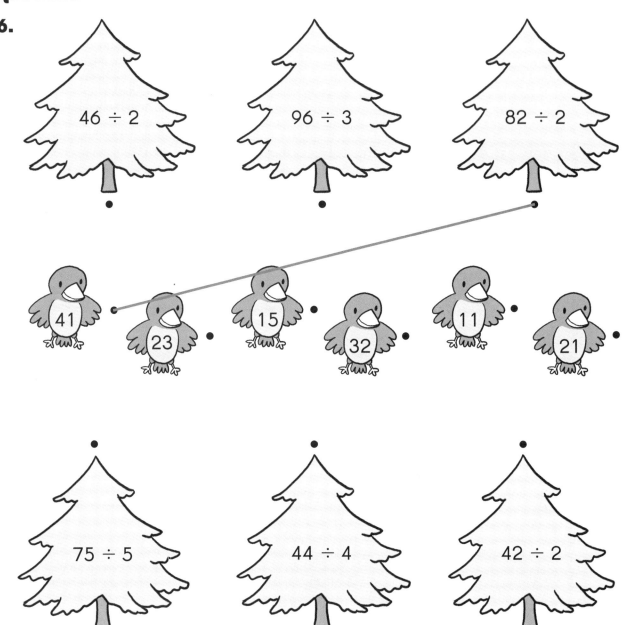

$46 \div 2$

$96 \div 3$

$82 \div 2$

41

23

15

32

11

21

$75 \div 5$

$44 \div 4$

$42 \div 2$

Practice 5　Division with Regrouping in Tens and Ones

Divide. Use base-ten blocks to help you.

1.
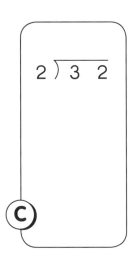

$2 \overline{)\ 3\ 2}$

Ⓒ

2.
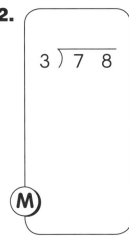

$3 \overline{)\ 7\ 8}$

Ⓜ

3.
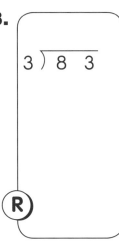

$3 \overline{)\ 8\ 3}$

Ⓡ

4.
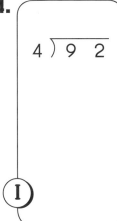

$4 \overline{)\ 9\ 2}$

Ⓘ

5.
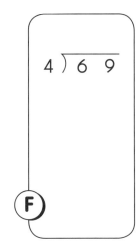

$4 \overline{)\ 6\ 9}$

Ⓕ

6.

$5 \overline{)\ 7\ 5}$

Ⓐ

7.

$5 \overline{)\ 6\ 3}$

Ⓣ

8.

$2 \overline{)\ 7\ 2}$

Ⓙ

What kind of jam cannot be eaten?

Match the letters to the quotients below to find out.

9.

———　———　———　———　———　———　———　　———　———　———
　12　　27　　15　　17　　17　　23　　16　　　36　　15　　26

Math Journal

Write *True* or *False*.
If the statement is false, rewrite the sentence to make it true.

1. When I divide one number by another, the answer is called a remainder. Any number left is called a quotient.

   _____

   _____

   _____

2. When an odd number is divided by 2, there is no remainder.

   _____

   _____

3. When an even number is divided by 2, there is a remainder.

   _____

   _____

4. I always divide the ones first, then the tens for the following:

   $3\overline{)3\ 2}$ $\qquad$ $4\overline{)2\ 6}$ $\qquad$ $5\overline{)7\ 1}$

   _____

   _____

Put On Your Thinking Cap!

Challenging Practice

Solve.

1. Find the sum of all the odd numbers between 60 and 66.

2. Which of these division statements are true?
Color them.

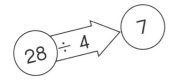

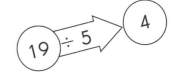

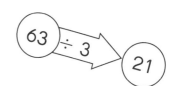

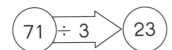

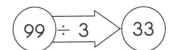

Put On Your Thinking Cap!

Problem Solving

Solve.

Mrs. Jones has some coloring books to give away as gifts.
She has fewer than 60 but more than 40 coloring books.
She will have 2 coloring books left over if she divides them equally among
10 children.
She will also have 2 coloring books left over if she divides them equally
among 8 children.
How many coloring books does she have?

Use the table to help you.
**Check (✓) or cross (✗) the last column to show whether the answer
is correct.**
The first two rows are done for you.

Number of Coloring Books	Divide Among 10 Children	Divide Among 8 Children	Correct ?
59	5 R 9	7 R 3	✗
52	5 R 2	6 R 4	✗
48			

Mrs. Jones has _____ coloring books.

Using Bar Models: Multiplication and Division

Chapter 9

Practice 1 Real-World Problems: Multiplication

Solve. Use bar models to help you.

Example

Carlos bakes 42 muffins.
Kim bakes twice as many muffins as Carlos.
How many muffins does Kim bake?

42 muffins

Carlos

Kim

?

$42 \times 2 =$ ___*84*___

Kim bakes ___*84*___ muffins.

1. Mrs. Bently pays $95 for a new bed.
   Mrs. Lee pays three times as much as Mrs. Bently for a new bed.
   How much does Mrs. Lee pay for the new bed?

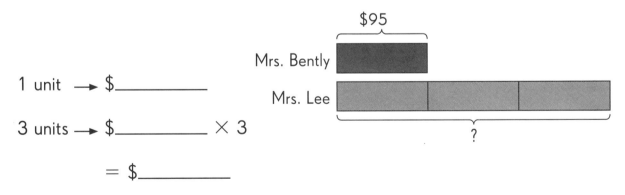

$95

Mrs. Bently

Mrs. Lee

?

1 unit ⟶ $_____

3 units ⟶ $_____ × 3

= $_____

Mrs. Lee pays $_____ for a new bed.

Solve. Draw bar models to help you.

2.   Mr. Suarez drove 98 miles on his vacation this year.
He drove 4 times that distance last year.
How far did Mr. Suarez drive on his vacation last year?

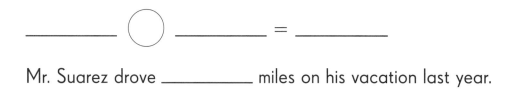

Mr. Suarez drove _____ miles on his vacation last year.

3.   School A collects 76 bundles of newspaper for recycling.
School B collects 5 times the number of bundles as School A.
How many bundles of newspaper does School B collect?

Practice 2   Real-World Problems:
Two-step Problems with Multiplication

Solve. Draw bar models to help you.

Example

6 boys and 4 girls are in the chorus.
Each chorus member has 8 concert tickets to sell.

a. How many members are in the chorus?

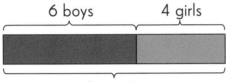

6 boys   4 girls

? members

_____6_____ (+) _____4_____ = _____10_____

There are _____10_____ members in the chorus.

b. How many concert tickets do they have in all?

8 tickets

? concert tickets

_____10_____ (×) _____8_____ = _____80_____

They have _____80_____ concert tickets in all.

Solve. Draw bar models to help you.

1. The school cafeteria sells 88 cartons of milk in a month.
It sells 4 times as many bottles of water.

   a. How many bottles of water does the cafeteria sell?

_____ ◯ _____ = _____

The cafeteria sells _____ bottles of water.

   b. How many more bottles of water than cartons of milk
does the cafeteria sell?

_____ ◯ _____ = _____

The cafeteria sells _____ more bottles of water than
cartons of milk.

Solve. Draw bar models to help you.

2. A museum has 75 carvings in its collection.
It has 10 more pieces of pottery than carvings.
It has 3 times as many paintings as pieces of pottery.
How many paintings does the museum have?

First, I _____.

Then, I _____.

3.   The second graders collect 65 books for the book drive.
They put some of the books in boxes and have 25 books left to pack.
The third graders have 4 times as many books in boxes.
There are none left to pack.
How many books do the third graders collect?

First, I _____.

Then, I _____.

Solve. Draw bar models to help you.

4.   Mary has 215 pencils.
She wants to put 30 pencils in 8 boxes.
How many more pencils does she need?

5. A bookcase has 5 shelves.
Each shelf has 120 books.
174 books are fiction.
How many books are nonfiction?

Solve. Use bar models to help you.

6. Eunice reads 5 times as many pages as Peter.
Kevin reads 30 more pages than Eunice.
Peter reads 25 pages.
How many pages does Kevin read?

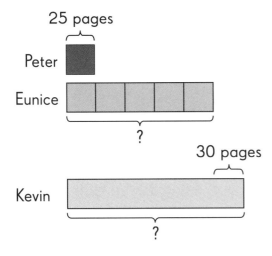

1 unit ⟶ _____

5 units ⟶ _____ ◯ _____

= _____

Eunice reads _____ pages.

_____ ◯ _____ = _____

Kevin reads _____ pages.

Solve. Draw bar models to help you.

7.   Jill has 28 stickers.
Peggy has 4 times as many stickers as Jill.
Luis has 15 fewer stickers than Peggy.
How many stickers does Luis have?

Practice 3   Real-World Problems: Division

Solve. Use bar models to help you.

Example

May has 48 flowers.
She needs 4 flowers to make each centerpiece.
How many such centerpieces can she make?

48 flowers

? centerpieces

$\underline{\quad 48 \quad} \div \underline{\quad 4 \quad} = \underline{\quad 12 \quad}$

She can make ____12____ such centerpieces.

---

1.   Mr. Morton shares 75 marbles equally among 5 children.
How many marbles does each child get?

75 marbles

?

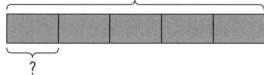

$\underline{\qquad} \div \underline{\qquad} = \underline{\qquad}$

Each child gets _____ marbles.

Solve. Use bar models to help you.

2.   Cally works 63 hours in 7 weeks.
She works an equal number of hours per week.
How many hours does she work per week?

_____ ◯ _____ = _____

She works _____ hours per week.

3.   Each shirt has 8 buttons.
There are 72 buttons in all.
How many shirts are there?

_____ ◯ _____ = _____

There are _____ shirts.

Solve. Use bar models to help you.

Example

Tina gives $85 to Aiden and Nick.
Aiden gets 4 times as much money as Nick.
How much does Nick get?

Aiden [| | |]
Nick [   ]   } $85

5 units ———→ $____85____

1 unit ———→ $____85____ (÷) ____5____

= $____17____

Nick gets $____17____.

4. Auntie Agnes makes 24 hot dogs.
She puts them on a round tray and a square tray.
Twice as many hot dogs are on the square tray as on the round tray.
How many more hot dogs are there on the square tray than on the round tray?

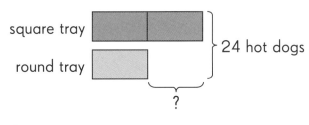

3 units ———→ _____

1 unit ———→ _____ ◯ _____

= _____

There are _____ more hot dogs on the square tray.

Solve. Draw bar models to help you.

5.   Elena takes 80 photos on her vacation.
        She takes 4 times as many photos as Luke.
        How many photos does Luke take?

6.   Mr. King picked 54 peaches from his orchard.
        He picked 9 times as many peaches as Mr. Tang.
        How many peaches did Mr. Tang pick?

Practice 4   Real-World Problems: Two-step Problems with Division

Solve. Use bar models to help you.

Example

Katie bakes 56 pineapple tarts.
She packs 20 pineapple tarts into a plastic container.
The remaining tarts are packed equally into 6 boxes.

a. How many pineapple tarts are packed into boxes?

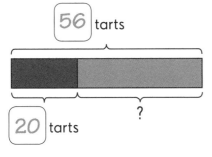

56   (−)   20   =   36

_____36_____ pineapple tarts are packed into boxes.

b. How many pineapple tarts are in each box?

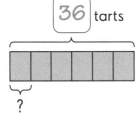

36   (÷)   6   =   6

There are ____6____ pineapple tarts in each box.

Solve. Use bar models to help you.

1. A fruit seller has 64 oranges in some bags.
Each bag has 8 oranges.
She sells the oranges for $2 per bag.
How much does she sell all the oranges for?

64 oranges

| 8 | | 8 |

? bags of oranges

How many bags of
oranges are there?

First, I _____.

Then, I _____.

_____ ◯ _____ = _____

There are _____ bags of oranges.

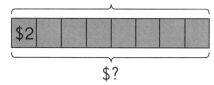

bags of oranges

| $2 | | | | | | | |

$?

_____ ◯ _____ = _____

She sells all the oranges for $ _____.

Solve. Draw bar models to help you.

2. Lance and Alex have 70 pencils.
Lance has 4 times as many pencils as Alex.
Alex's pencils are shared equally among 2 children.
How many pencils does each child get?

First, I _____.

Then, I _____.

3. Richard has 90 pennies.
He keeps 10 pennies and divides the rest
of the pennies equally among his 4 sisters.
How many pennies does each sister get?

First, I _____.

Then, I _____.

Solve. Draw bar models to help you.

4.   A baker makes 32 rolls in the morning.
He makes 64 rolls in the afternoon. He packs all the rolls equally into 4 boxes.
How many rolls does each box have?

5.   Marcus collects 14 stamps each month.
Wayne collects 19 stamps each month.
How many months does Wayne take to collect 65 stamps more than Marcus?

 Math Journal

Look at the bar models, number sentences, and the answer statement. Write a question that matches this problem.

1.

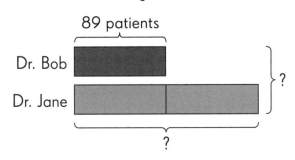

89 patients

Dr. Bob

Dr. Jane

?

?

$3 \times 89 = 89 \times 3$

Method 1

$89 \times 2 = 178$ or

$178 + 89 = 267$

Method 2

1 unit ⟶ 89

3 units ⟶ $3 \times 89 = 267$

Both doctors see 267 patients.

My question:

**Look at the bar models and the answer statement.
Write a question that matches this problem and
show two possible methods for solving the word problem.**

2.

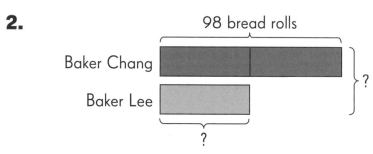

98 bread rolls

Baker Chang

Baker Lee

?

?

Both bakers bake 147 bread rolls.

My question:

My methods:

Name: _____ Date: _____

 Put On Your Thinking Cap!

 Challenging Practice

Solve. Draw bar models to help you.

Timmy and Pedro have 24 trading cards altogether.
Timmy gives Pedro 5 cards, and they each have the
same number of cards.
How many trading cards does Pedro have at first?

Put On Your Thinking Cap!

Problem Solving

Solve. Use bar models to help you.

Johanna has some chicken nuggets and 6 sticks.

She puts 3 chicken nuggets on each stick.

She has 2 chicken nuggets left.

If she puts 4 chicken nuggets on each stick,

how many chicken nuggets will be left?

How many sticks will she need?

Cumulative Review

for Chapters 8 and 9

Concepts and Skills

Complete. Use the digits 1, 3, and 8. *(Lesson 8.3)*

1. Write two 3-digit even numbers.

even numbers
_____
_____

2. Write four 3-digit odd numbers.

odd numbers	
_____	_____
_____	_____

Fill in the blanks. Use mental math. *(Lesson 8.1)*

3. $6 \div 2 =$ _____

$60 \div 2 =$ _____ tens $\div$ 2

$=$ _____ tens

$=$ _____

$600 \div 2 =$ _____ hundreds $\div$ 2

$=$ _____ hundreds

$=$ _____

Divide. *(Lessons 8.4 and 8.5)*

4. $3\overline{)9\ \ 6}$ **5.** $3\overline{)9\ \ 3}$ **6.** $5\overline{)5\ \ 6}$

7. $2\overline{)7\ \ 3}$ **8.** $4\overline{)4\ \ 7}$ **9.** $5\overline{)9\ \ 8}$

Divide. Then match the division facts that have the same quotients. *(Lessons 8.1 and 8.2)*

10. $35 \div 5$ •   • $180 \div 4$

        $27 \div 3$ •   • $56 \div 8$

        $135 \div 3$ •   • $36 \div 4$

        $75 \div 5$ •   • $96 \div 3$

        $64 \div 2$ •   • $15 \div 1$

Problem Solving

Solve. Draw bar models to help you.

11. Roland has 125 trading cards.
Ian has three times as many trading cards as Roland.
How many trading cards does Ian have?

12. Mr. Hansen gives out 250 pencils to 5 classes.
Each class receives an equal number of pencils.
How many pencils does each class receive?

13. Mike is three times as tall as Pamela.
Pamela is 2 feet tall.

    a. How tall is Mike?

    b. How many feet taller is Mike than Pamela?

14. Mrs. Herra buys 3 boxes of oranges. She also buys 6 boxes of apples.
Each box contains 65 pieces of fruit.

    a. How many boxes of fruit does Mrs. Herra buy?

    b. How many pieces of fruit does Mrs. Herra buy?

Name: _____ **Date:** _____

15. Shaun has 96 ounces of lemonade.
He pours all the lemonade equally into 6 jugs.
He then pours out one of the jugs of lemonade to fill 2 glasses.
How many ounces of lemonade does each glass hold?

16. A watch costs $56.
A camera costs double the amount of the watch.
How much do the two items cost in all?

17. Ben has 4 cartons of crayons.
Each carton contains 120 crayons.
He puts them equally into 6 cartons.
How many crayons are in each carton?

18. Natalie has 275 centimeters of ribbon to make headbands.
She makes 4 headbands and has 15 centimeters of ribbon left.
What length of ribbon does she use for each headband?

Name: _____   Date: _____

Mid-Year Review

Test Prep

Multiple Choice

Fill in the circle next to the correct answer.

1. In the number 6,592, the digit 5 is in the __Hundred__ ⁺ place. *(Lesson 1.2)*

     Ⓐ ones   Ⓑ tens

     Ⓒ (hundreds)   Ⓓ thousands

2. Which number is 1,000 more than 1,629? *(Lesson 1.3)*

     Ⓐ 629   Ⓑ 1,619

     Ⓒ (1,729)   Ⓓ 2,629

3. Estimate the sum of 342 and 525. Use front-end estimation. *(Lesson 2.5)*

     Ⓐ 300 + 500 = 800   Ⓑ (300 + 530 = 830)

     Ⓒ 340 + 500 = 840   Ⓓ 340 + 530 = 870

4. Estimate the difference between 828 and 535.
Use rounding to the nearest hundred. *(Lesson 2.4)*

     Ⓐ 900 − 500 = 400

     Ⓑ 800 − 500 = 300

     Ⓒ 900 − 600 = 300

     (Ⓓ) 800 − 600 = 200

$$342$$
$$525+$$
$$\overline{867}$$

$$300$$
$$530+$$
$$\overline{830}$$

5. $0 \times 9 =$ _____ *(Lesson 6.1)*

(A) 0   (B) 9

(C) 90   (D) 900

6. To find the answer to 38 + 48, You can add 50 to ___50___.
(Lesson 2.1)

(A) 38, then add 2   (B) 38, then subtract 2

(C) 48, then add 2   (D) 48, then subtract 2

7. What is the missing digit? *(Lesson 3.3)*

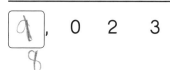
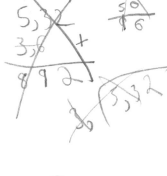

```
   5,  3  2  [61]
 + 3,  6  [0]  4
 _____
   [9], 0  2  3
      8
```

(A) 1   (B) 2

(C) 5   (D) 9

8. There are four numbers on a whiteboard:

1,390, 1,125, 1,580, and 1,625.

The difference between two of the numbers is 235.

What are the two numbers? *(Lesson 4.3)*

(A) 1,580 and 1,390   (B) 1,625 and 1,390

(C) 1,390 and 1,125   (D) 1,580 and 1,125

9. How many numbers between 31 and 50 can be
divided by 6 with no remainder? *(Lesson 8.4)*

(A) 1 (B) 2

(C) 3 (D) 4

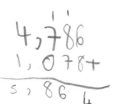

4,786
1,078+
5,864

10. Add 4,786 and 1,078. *(Lesson 3.3)*

(A) 3,708 (B) 3,808

(C) 5,764 (D) 5,864

11. Subtract 1,786 from 3,000. *(Lesson 4.3)*

(A) 1,204 (B) 1,214

(C) 2,786 (D) 4,786

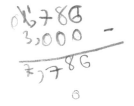

3,000
1,786 -
1,786

12. 215 × 4 = _____. *(Lesson 7.3)*

(A) 172 (B) 211

(C) 219 (D) 860

215
4 ×
0,842

13. Which of the following is the same as 5 × 9? *(Lesson 6.5)*

(A) 9 + 5 (B) 5 + 5 + 9 + 9

(C) 5 + 5 + 5 + 5 + 5 (D) 9 + 9 + 9 + 9 + 9

14. Drew has 87 pebbles.
He divides the pebbles equally into 3 bags.
How many pebbles does he have in each bag? *(Lesson 8.5)*

(A) 29   (B) 84

(C) 90   (D) 261

15. The sum of two numbers is 100.
The difference between the two numbers is 26.
What is the number that is less? *(Lesson 5.1)*

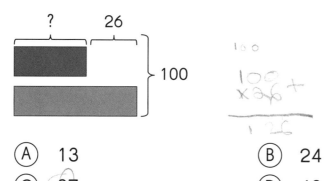

(A) 13   (B) 24

(C) 37   (D) 63

Short Answer

**Read the questions carefully.
Write each answer in the space provided.**

16. Write three thousand, fourteen in standard form. *(Lesson 1.1)*

3,14

17. What is the value of the digit 5 in the number 5,631? *(Lesson 1.2)*

hundrids

18. Use the digits below to make three 3-digit odd numbers and three 3-digit even numbers. Do not repeat the same digits in a number. *(Lesson 8.3)*

1   8   2   3   9   4   7

Odd numbers: _2 3944 397_

Even numbers: _24 8_

19. Add 1,850 + 59. *(Lesson 3.2)*

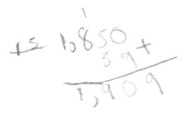

_1,909_

20. 70 × 4 = ? *(Lesson 7.1)*

$$\begin{array}{r} 70 \\ \times\ 4 \\ \hline 284 \end{array}$$

_＊ ＊ 284_

21. In 59 ÷ 2, the quotient is ___59＃___, and the remainder is ___4___. *(Lesson 8.2)*

22. Shaun takes 300 photographs at the zoo.
Sheena takes twice as many photographs as Shaun.
How many photographs do they take in all? *(Lesson 9.1)*

300 · 300   600
2x   2+   306+
___   ___
600   302   900

_____ photos

23. Shannon has 78 animal stickers.
She has three times as many animal stickers as her brother, Ryan.
How many animal stickers does Ryan have? *(Lesson 9.3)*

3)78

26

_____ paperclips

24. The sum of two numbers is 1,500.
The difference between these two numbers is 300.
Find these two numbers from the numbers provided. *(Lessons 3.2 and 4.1)*

123 x **1,200   600   300   700   800   900**

600 and 900
_____

25. Caroline packs some glue sticks into 8 bags.
She has 12 glue sticks left over.
If there are 25 glue sticks in each bag, how many
glue sticks did she have at first? *(Lessons 7.3 and 3.1)*

25   8   12
+8   12   25
         12+
          8

_____

26.   What is the product of 1 × 7 × 2?
Use the number lines to help you. *(Lessons 6.1 and 6.2)*

1 × 7 × 2 = 1 × _____

= _____

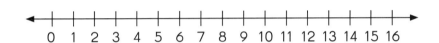

1 × 7 × 2 = _____ × 2

= _____

So, 1 × _____ = _____ × 2

= _____.

27. Find the sum of 938 and 8,163. *(Lesson 3.3)*

_____

28. Find the difference between 6,215 and 8,356. *(Lesson 4.3)*

_____

29. Find the product of 154 and 4. *(Lesson 7.3)*

_____

30. Use the digits below to form two 2-digit numbers.
Each number has a remainder of 1 when divided by 4. *(Lesson 8.2)*

1   3   7   9

_____

31. Find the difference between 45 ÷ 5 and 5 × 7. *(Lessons 4.3, 6.3, and 7.1)*

_____

32. Use the model. How many stamps does Alex have? *(Lesson 5.1)*

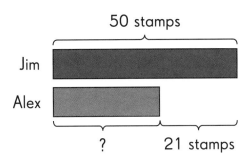

                                        _____ stamps

33. A craft store sells 1,124 fewer pieces of red art paper
than blue art paper.
It sells 2,317 pieces of red art paper.
How many pieces of red and blue art paper does the craft store sell?
(Lessons 3.3 and 4.3)

                                        _____ pieces

34. Ngu walks 250 feet.
She walks 65 feet more than Pauline.
How far does Pauline walk? *(Lesson 4.3)*

                                        _____ feet

35. Oomi makes 4 necklaces.
She uses 156 beads for each necklace.
How many beads does she use in all? *(Lesson 7.3)*

                                        _____ beads

Extended Response

Solve. Show your work.

36. Jolene has 600 wooden beads.
She has 285 fewer glass beads than wooden beads.

a. How many glass beads does Jolene have?

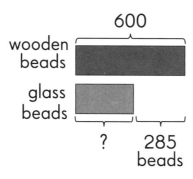

b. How many wooden beads does she have if she uses 150 of them to make necklaces?

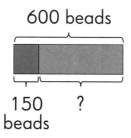

37.   Company A gets 3,700 hits on their website.
Company B gets 450 fewer hits than Company A.

a.   How many hits does Company B get?

b.   How many hits do both companies get in all?

38. Noah swims 80 laps in 5 days.
He swims the same number of laps every day.
a. How many laps does he swim in a day?

b. How many laps does he swim in 4 days?

39. Jose has 88 stickers.
He puts 4 stickers on each bookmark.
He gives all his bookmarks away to his friends.
Each friend receives 2 bookmarks.

a. How many bookmarks does he put stickers on?

b. How many friends does he have?

40. A factory delivers 5 containers of pottery to a store.
Each container has 162 pieces of pottery.
The store owner discovers 24 pieces of pottery are broken.
How many pieces of pottery are not broken?